THE CHANGING FACE OF
CHINA

Text by STEPHEN KEELER
Photography by CHRIS FAIRCLOUGH

WAYLAND

Produced for Hodder Wayland by

White-Thomson Publishing Ltd

2/3 St Andrew's Place

Lewes

BN7 1UP

Editor: Alison Cooper
Designer: Christopher Halls at Mind's Eye Design, Lewes
Proofreader: Philippa Smith
Additional picture research: Shelley Noronha, Glass Onion Pictures

Published in Great Britain in 2002 by Hodder Wayland, an imprint of
Hodder Children's Books

This paperback edition published by Wayland in 2007,
an imprint of Hachette Children's Books.

British Library Cataloguing in Publication Data
Keeler, Stephen
  Changing Face of China
  1. China - Juvenile literature
  I. Title II. China
    951

ISBN-10: 0 7502 3852 6
ISBN-13: 978 0 7502 3852 6

Printed and bound in China

Wayland,
an imprint of Hachette Children's Books
338 Euston Rd, London NW1 3BH

Acknowledgements

The author, photographer and publishers are grateful to all those who agreed to be interviewed and photographed for this book. Special thanks, for their very generous assistance, to: Mr Jiang Dengzhen of Xi'an Foreign Languages University; Humphrey Keenlyside of the China–Britain Business Council; Professor Rao Dujun of the Shaanxi Province Foreign Affairs Office; Mr William Zhang, Beijing; Mr Hua Ning of the Embassy of the People's Republic of China, London. The publisher would also like to thank the following for their contribution: Rob Bowden – statistics research; Nick Hawken – statistic panel illustrations; Peter Bull – map illustration. All photographs are by Chris Fairclough except: Eye Ubiquitous 23/Julia Waterlow; Wayland Picture Library 10, 13/Gordon Clements, 17 (top and centre), 22 (top), 30 (bottom); Impact 12 (top)/Christophe Bluntzer, 22 (bottom) /Mark Henley; Popperfoto/Reuters 14, 45.

Contents

1 Shanghai – China's Oriental Pearl

Nowhere on the planet are there more construction sites than in Shanghai, China's second city. Everywhere there are new office blocks, shopping streets, apartments, elevated highways, wharves and bridges. Work is underway on the Shanghai World Financial Centre, which will be the world's tallest building when completed. This booming city is older, bigger, more fashionable and even more successful in business than its southern neighbour, Hong Kong.

▲ *Shanghai's growing importance as a centre for business is reflected in the number of skyscrapers that crowd the city skyline.*

The changes that have transformed Shanghai have taken place very recently. For generations, China resisted contact with the outside world. While other countries were developing their industries and building up trading links, China's industry stagnated, its agriculture remained primitive and its people were poor.

All that is changing. China is rapidly becoming one of the world's major trading nations and evidence of this can be seen in Shanghai. People are better off than ever and keen to spend their income on the new consumer products. As recently as the 1980s the ambition of most Chinese was to own a watch, a sewing machine and a bicycle. Today's young Chinese have much higher expectations.

▶ *These shop workers from Suzhou have little money to spend on clothes and CDs but they go window-shopping in nearby Shanghai whenever they can.*

▲ *China's major landscape features and the towns and regions mentioned in this book.*

CHINA: KEY FACTS

Area: 9,572,900 sq km

Population: 1,295.33 million

Population density: 130 people per sq km

Capital city: Beijing (12.5 million)

Other major cities: Shanghai (7.5 million); Hong Kong (7.25 million); Tianjin (4.5 million); Shenyang (4 million); Wuhan (3.25 million); Guangzhou (3 million)

Highest mountain: Chu-mu-lang-ma Feng (Everest) – 8,848 m

Longest river: Yangtze (6,300 km)

Main languages: Chinese (Mandarin or *Putonghua*; Cantonese; Wu)

Main religions: Taoism (20%); Buddhism (8.5%); Christianity (6%); Muslim (1.4%)

Currency: Renminbi (People's Currency) – 10 fen = 1 jiao, 10 jiao = 1 yuan

2 Past Times

Five thousand years of history

The earliest human communities in China developed in neolithic times, around 5,000 years ago, near the present-day cities of Xi'an, Chengdu and Wuhan. In this area, people built defensive walls around their homes and made domestic pottery. Populations grew and slowly spread towards the south and east of the country. They cultivated wheat and millet and farmed silkworms to make fabric for clothing.

Eventually, powerful families, known as dynasties, emerged as rulers. The first dynasty, the Xia, ruled about 4,000 years ago. By around 2000 BC the Zhou Dynasty had introduced a civil service to administer the region. Iron was invented and coins were first used for trading. But it was a period of racial and political unrest. Most Chinese were peasants who lived brutal lives in desperate poverty.

◀ Qin Shi Huangdi's 'terracotta army', rediscovered near Xi'an in 1974. After Beijing and the Great Wall, this is China's third most visited tourist attraction.

IN THEIR OWN WORDS

'My name is Ke Li and I live in Wuhan. I've been studying calligraphy for ten years now, but you never finish studying calligraphy. It's a lifetime's work. I write out Tang Dynasty poems – about walking in the mountains, for example – and sell them, mostly to tourists. The Tang Dynasty [618–907] was a golden era for Chinese literature – the poetry is beautiful. It's good when it flows from the heart and the words feel deep and strong on the paper. Each word must have its own identity. Brushes have to be hand-made; the hair is from wolves or bears. The ink is pine resin mixed with water and powdered stone. Americans and Japanese pay a lot of money for my work. It's like being paid for doing your hobby. I'm going to buy a small house soon. My father can't believe it. No one in our family's history has ever owned a building.'

Qin Shi Huangdi was the first 'emperor' to unify all the warring rivals into one state – China (a name derived from *Qin*). He ruled between 221 and 206 BC and began the project to build the Great Wall. He was buried near his imperial capital city of Xi'an, with 7,000 life-size terracotta warriors.

During the Ming Dynasty (1368–1644) the Great Wall was repaired, rebuilt and completed. Techniques were developed for making exquisite blue and white pottery vases – or 'china', as Europeans began to call it.

The last dynasty to rule China was the Qing (1644–1911). Towards the end of this period, during the nineteenth century, floods and earthquakes devastated the country. These natural disasters repeatedly destroyed agriculture, demolished entire towns and disrupted international trade. Millions of Chinese died, many of them from starvation.

▶ *The Great Wall of China is 6,350 km long. Begun in 214 BC, its purpose was to protect China from Mongol invaders from the north.*

Revolution!

Under the last Qing emperors China became politically weak. Britain took over Hong Kong (1842), France occupied Vietnam (1858) and Taiwan was given to Japan (1895). Meanwhile, as their country was being torn apart by war, natural disasters and economic collapse, ordinary Chinese people continued to live in terrible poverty. Dissatisfaction and anger eventually led to a series of attempted revolutions.

◀ *These elderly people have witnessed a tumultuous period in China's history. They have lived through war and civil war, the setting up of the Communist state and the move towards greater economic and personal freedoms.*

Sun Yatsen announced the creation of the first Chinese republic on 1 January 1912, but Japan occupied northern China, including Beijing, and began to rule the country. Mao Zedong, the leader of the Communists, marched his supporters thousands of kilometres from the south to defeat the Japanese. He proclaimed the People's Republic of China on 1 October 1949 and ruled as 'Chairman' until his death in 1976.

Under Mao, all private land was seized by the state. State-owned farms known as collectives were set up, where peasants worked to provide food for the country's starving population. Industry, too, was nationalized. Personal freedom, as understood in the West, was unknown in Communist China.

Criticism of the government was not tolerated. China closed its doors to the outside world.

Mao Zedong was a charismatic leader who carried out great social reforms. He hated privilege and private wealth and worked for continuous change. In 1966 he led the Chinese student population in protests – which became known as the Cultural Revolution – against leading members of his own Communist Party. Since his death the regime has gradually relaxed. But progress has been frustratingly slow for young people, many of whom demonstrated against Communism in Tian An Men Square during the summer of 1989. The demonstration was brutally put down by the army.

▲ *A portrait of Mao Zedong still hangs over the Gateway of Heavenly Peace in Tian An Men Square, Beijing.*

IN THEIR OWN WORDS

'I'm Chen Ren, and I'm the lead singer in a rock band, *Red Flag Flying*. Our parents weren't supposed to dance or listen to Western music – not even classical music. My uncle was a journalist. A workmate reported him to the Communist Party for listening to the Voice of America radio station and he lost his job. He spent the Cultural Revolution working in the fields in Gansu province. He died there. We never saw him again.

Now we've all got radios and CD players. I got a mobile phone last year. I want to get a computer so I can find out more about Western bands and make lots of contacts on the Internet. We like British music from the late 1960s but we play Chinapop. I think we could sell millions of CDs outside China.'

Landscape and Climate

China is the world's third-largest country, after Canada and Russia. A little larger than the United States, China is roughly the size of all the countries of Europe put together. It shares borders with 14 countries and stretches across 60 lines of longitude and 25 lines of latitude. Its land borders stretch for 19,480 km, and it has a coastline some 13,920 km long. Yet it is principally a land of dust, sand, stone, rock and mountain. Only one-eighth of its land surface is suitable for agriculture.

North-east China

This region is made up of the provinces of Heilongjiang, Jilin and Liaoning. They are bordered by mountain ranges to the north and open to the sea to the east. Winters are long, dry and very cold, with an average temperature of –17 °C. In the short summer the average temperature is 23 °C. The average annual rainfall is around 400 mm.

▼ *The Yellow river flows through the desert in Ningxia in western China.*

Central China

Shanxi and Shaanxi provinces are densely populated in comparison to the rest of China. The land is rich in yellow loess soil brought down by the winds from the Gobi Desert. Together with Hebei and Shandong provinces, Shanxi and Shaanxi have cold, dry winters with an average temperature of –7 °C. Summers are hot and humid, with the average temperature reaching 28 °C. Average annual rainfall is around 450 mm. Much of China's old heavy industry, such as mining and steel production, is located in this region, along the Yellow River and around Greater Beijing. The Great Wall crosses the northern part of the region, and beyond it are the grasslands of Inner Mongolia.

▲ *The mountains of north-west Shaanxi province.*

IN THEIR OWN WORDS

'My name is Wang Bin and I have a farm in Shaanxi province. Good farmland is in short supply in China, so we farmers have to make the most of the land we've got. They even used to grow winter wheat along the top of the old city walls in Xi'an until just a few years ago. We cut terraces into the hillsides to give us more flat land to cultivate. You can't grow grain high up mountainsides, it's too cold and too difficult to reach. Here it's fairly flat and my land is rich loess – very good for grain, even tea and cotton. In a good year we live well, but when the floods come we can lose everything. Since the government gave us our own land to farm we don't get the same help from the state when times are tough. Nowadays you have to look after yourself.'

Highland plateau

The Western Chinese Plateau is the largest highland region in the world and covers over one-third of China's entire land surface. It includes Qinghai province and the autonomous regions of Xinjiang and Tibet, which is known as the 'roof of the world', in the south. Less than 3 per cent of the population – about three inhabitants per square km – live in this vast and relatively isolated area. Average winter temperatures are around –20 °C; average summer temperatures are around 20 °C. Rainfall averages around 150 mm per year.

▲ *The barren landscape around Flaming Mountain, in Xinjiang.*

IN THEIR OWN WORDS

'I am Sun Jiaoyang. I live in Gansu province, in the north-west. Around Lanzhou there's plenty of good farmland but there are mountains to the south and west and desert in the north. There aren't many big towns in this region and a lot of the villages are very isolated. That's why my job is so important. I'm what is known as a 'barefoot doctor'. I'm not an expert – I couldn't do a surgical operation – but I am qualified in basic medical procedures. I can stitch a bad wound, remove a rotten tooth, deliver babies, inoculate children, treat most illnesses and handle emergencies. For many people, the nearest hospital is over 500 km away, so when I turn up in my jeep it's a big relief. When I first started I only had a bag of herbs and a strong bike! Now I have a mobile phone and a computer, as well as the jeep.'

The south-west

The south-west includes Sichuan, Yunnan and Guizhou provinces, where there are large populations of the Puyi, Yi, Hui and Tibetan ethnic groups. Sichuan – well known for its hot, spicy food – is densely populated and heavily industrialized. The climate of this region is sub-tropical, with an average annual rainfall of around 720 mm, mainly falling during the summer months of April to August. Kunming, in Yunnan province, is known as the 'City of Eternal Spring' because it has a stable, temperate climate, even though it is almost 2,000 m above sea-level.

The south

China's second and third cities – Shanghai and Guangzhou – are located in the south. The Yangtze and Pearl rivers flow through this region and the climate is tropical, with average winter temperatures of 8 °C and summer averages of around 31 °C. The average rainfall is around 1,000 mm per year and short, heavy tropical storms are frequent.

► *A woman returning from the country market, near Guilin in Guanxi province, southern China. The 'sugar-loaf' rock formations in the distance are typical of this region.*

Natural Resources

Energy

China has around 115 billion tonnes of coal – these are the world's third-largest reserves, after those of the USA and Russia. However, as the largest deposits are in the north of the country, much of China's coal has to be transported long distances to other industrial regions in the centre and south-east. Transporting coal is slow, costly and inefficient.

▲ *Coal produced in this mine is used to generate electricity in the power station next door.*

Coal-burning produces levels of environmental pollution which are no longer acceptable.

China's other energy sources include large oil reserves, which are estimated to contain 24 billion barrels of oil – about the same level of reserves as those of the USA. It also uses water from some of its great rivers to generate electricity. The Three Gorges Dam, on the Yangtze River, in Hubei province, is the

▼ *A construction site on the Three Gorges Dam. The project is due for completion in 2009.*

world's largest. Its reservoir is 650 km long. Over a million people will be moved to new homes and numerous important archaeological sites will be flooded during its construction. Its hydroelectric power station will reduce China's need for heavily polluting coal-fired power stations. However, many people are strongly opposed to the project because of the damage it will cause to the environment during construction.

Water

Over 400 Chinese cities suffer from water shortages, costing the economy around US$ 14.5 billion a year. Less than 15 per cent of waste water is treated or recycled. China's Academy of Engineering estimates that the country will suffer serious water shortages by 2030, when the population is expected to peak at 1.6 billion.

Many city authorities are investing in improved water-pumping systems. There are numerous projects to transport water through an impressive network of underground pipes. New reservoirs such as the one being created behind the Three Gorges Dam should also help to boost water supplies. However, China is a massive country with a huge population and relatively low rainfall. Water shortages are likely to remain a problem for the foreseeable future.

IN THEIR OWN WORDS

'My name is Xiao He. I'm 72 years old and I've certainly seen some changes in my lifetime. Life is more comfortable today – perhaps not better, but more comfortable. There are no more food shortages – not here in Wuhan anyway. I've still got a ration book for cotton cloth, but that doesn't matter; I don't make my own clothes now, I buy them. But the water – now, that is a problem. We still have no water in our part of town on most Wednesdays and sometimes none on Saturdays either. The factories need it and production can't stop, so we get rationed. We are used to it but I have to remember to fill half a dozen buckets on Tuesday nights.'

Farming for self-sufficiency

Agricultural land is scarce in China. The country has only 7 per cent of the world's arable land, yet it has to feed almost a quarter of the world's population. Farms are generally no longer large, state-owned collectives; they are small businesses, run by single households. However, to improve their efficiency farmers often co-operate, sharing labour and the costs of expensive machinery. They still have to supply food to the government, but once they have supplied the government quota they are allowed to sell any extra produce in the 'free' markets.

Agricultural output is impressive. China, which as recently as fifty years ago regularly suffered catastrophic famines, now produces the world's largest share of wheat, millet, rice, meat and meat products. It is the world's second-largest producer of tea and oilseed rape. Chinese farmers produce most of the world's silkworms and supply industry with over four million tonnes of cotton every year.

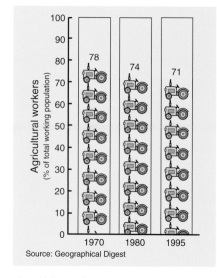

▲ Although the percentage of workers employed in agriculture is falling, they still make up more than two-thirds of the working population.

◄ Stallholders at a 'free' market in Shanghai. The best produce can usually be found in the free markets and prices are always higher than in markets organized by the local authorities.

◄ *Water buffalo are still used in rice paddies, where tractors cannot be used.*

▶ *A farmer taking his produce to market. Despite the rise in car ownership in cities, most people in the countryside still use bicycles and tricycles to get around.*

IN THEIR OWN WORDS

'I'm Sun Min Zhou and I'm a farmer in Sichuan. We grow maize and sweet potatoes. Everything's done by hand, and our days are long and hard. We own our farm and share ownership of a combine harvester with neighbouring farmers.

People are always talking about the environment these days. I have to grow crops under plastic and I have to use chemical fertilizers, otherwise this farm wouldn't produce enough to be worth farming. We have to produce enough for ourselves, to sell locally and to supply agreed quotas to the state. It's no picnic! When the plastic's finished I have to burn it or bury it – and no, it's not biodegradable. We couldn't afford stuff like that. Look, my priority is to support my family. If the politicians have a problem with the environment let the politicians solve it, not the farmers.'

The price of progress

China has been very successful in increasing the size of its harvests. Unfortunately, increases in agricultural production have partly depended on the intensive use of chemical fertilizers and pesticides. Many of these cause serious damage to the environment, damaging the soil in the long term and polluting water supplies. Some of the products that are still used in China have been banned for many years in Western countries.

China's agricultural land is also threatened by rapid urban expansion. The areas where most of the population live are also the areas where some of the best arable land is located. As China's industries expand, more homes have to be built for workers. More roads, schools and hospitals have to be built, too. All these building projects devour more precious land, produce domestic waste and increase traffic pollution.

▲ *It is estimated that almost half of China's population will live in urban areas by 2015.*

Source: UNDP/Geographical Digest

◄ *A tractor spreading chemical fertilizer on farmland in central Shaanxi province.*

Conserving China's wildlife

Pressure on land threatens not only China's farmers but also some of its rare wildlife. Conservation projects have been set up to try to protect threatened species but they do not always succeed. Back in 1975, the Wolong Nature Reserve was established in Sichuan province to protect about 150 of China's

IN THEIR OWN WORDS

'My name is William Zhang. I'm a journalist, based in Beijing. When I first visited London, about twenty years ago, I was curious to see the recycling logo for the first time. Now it's on every street corner in Beijing. The government is getting serious about environmental protection. Beijing City Council promoted a campaign called 'Bring back our blue sky' to reduce smog, mainly by insisting on the use of more refined coal and gas. I would say that, among China's urban population, the need to reduce air pollution is generally accepted.

The greatest threat to our environment is from changes in lifestyle. Giant shopping malls and hypermarkets are springing up everywhere. Families are becoming more middle class. They leave these places with armfuls of over-packaged goods. Imagine one and a quarter billion people all leaving the supermarket with a couple of plastic bags each!'

wild and seriously endangered pandas. By the early 1990s, however, there were fewer than 75 pandas at Wolong and today there could be as few as 65. What went wrong?

Wolong is mostly inhabited by ethnic minorities, who are not subject to the One-Child Policy (see pages 24–25). The local birth-rate is about double the national average. A growing population requires more space. Wolong is in a relatively poor part of China where many families choose to burn wood rather than buy electricity for heating and cooking. Deforestation and smoke pollution have destroyed much of the pandas' habitat. Ironically, the 850 or so wild pandas remaining in unprotected areas probably have a better chance of survival than the pandas of Wolong.

▼ *The rapid growth in traffic is blamed for the massive increase in pollution levels in China's cities.*

The Changing Population

From the country to the cities

One in every five people on the planet lives in China. More people speak Chinese than any other language. China's enormous population is both a strength and a weakness. It provides a huge, relatively cheap workforce, but it makes enormous demands on the country's ability to feed and house itself.

The percentage of the population living in cities increased from 25 per cent in 1990 to 35 per cent in 2000. Millions of peasants have moved from the countryside to well-paid but insecure labouring jobs on the thousands of construction projects in the cities. Population density in the cities of the east and south can reach 2,200 people per square km. By contrast, population density in the remote plateaux and steppes of the west can be under five people per square km.

One result of China's rapid urbanization has been the creation of two distinct social classes: the new rich – relatively young, well-educated, property-owning; and the unskilled poor – often illiterate and frequently exploited by unscrupulous employers. Migrant workers from ethnic minority or farming communities often fall outside the

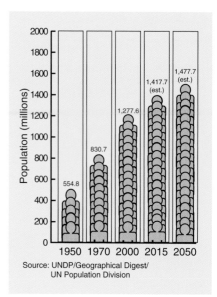

Source: UNDP/Geographical Digest/
UN Population Division

▲ China's population more than doubled in the second half of the twentieth century.

◀ A thicket of scaffolding poles covers a building site near Xi'an. Bamboo is traditionally used for scaffolding, although these poles are made of metal.

system of social welfare that provides for most Chinese citizens. The rapidly widening gap between rich and poor is a major cause of increasing social unrest. Such problems could threaten China's impressive economic growth and the stability of its government.

▶ *Apartment blocks in Guangzhou tower above older housing. The area at the front of the picture has been cleared in preparation for new building work.*

IN THEIR OWN WORDS

'My name is Guo Zhoujian and I live in Guangzhou. My parents were both civil engineers. They designed bridges, harbours and military bases. We lived well but we weren't rich. No one was rich in those days. Now I've just got my first job as a surveyor's assistant on a luxury development of three-storey apartments. They're like palaces. My parents wouldn't believe it!

I can afford a motor bike, something my father would have loved when he was my age. It's a Japanese design but made in China. I'm going to enjoy it while I can. The traffic pollution is so bad in Guangzhou now that the authorities are going to ban all motor cycles and any car over 15 years old from the city centre.'

Who are the Chinese?

Fifty-six officially recognized ethnic groups make up China's population. However, over 90 per cent of Chinese are ethnic Han – a name that originates from the time of the Han Dynasty (206 BC–AD 220), when the population of the central and eastern parts of the country began to share a language and culture. The Han looked on other ethnic groups – especially the sheep-herding nomadic peoples of the north and west – as foreigners. For many generations China's rulers have been sending large groups of Han to administer remoter regions, where some ethnic minorities number under 1,000.

The principal ethnic minorities include Mongols, Uighurs, Tibetans and Miao. Altogether, there are around 100 million ethnic-minority citizens.

▲ *These Tibetans are novice monks, from the lamasery at Lanzhou.*

◀ *A herder with his goats on the grasslands of Inner Mongolia.*

IN THEIR OWN WORDS

'I'm Mao Xin. I work in an office in Kunming. I'm a Miao, and the clothes I'm wearing are traditional Miao costume. They actually belong to my mother but I wear them now and again on special family occasions.

I don't really think about our ethnic origins very often. It was more of an issue for my parents. My father worked in a tea-packing factory all his life. He was a good worker and his colleagues respected him, but he never became a manager. If he'd been Han he would probably have become the director. When I was born my family had no close Han friends. But at school we mixed well and I don't think minorities would face discrimination today. If I find a boyfriend who's a Han it won't be a problem. We're all Chinese.'

Living on the fringes of modern China

At least 15 Chinese cities have populations of over two million. It is rare, though, to spot a foreign face in a Chinese crowd. Although many foreign business people now live and work in China's rapidly developing cities, mixed marriages between Chinese and non-Chinese are still rare enough to be controversial.

Even the majority of ethnic-minority citizens still live, literally, on the fringes of modern China, in the borderlands of 'outer' China. Unrest among ethnic-minority groups, especially the larger ones, could cause problems for the government. It therefore tries to avoid imposing policies on them that conflict with their culture and traditions. The One-Child Policy, for example, which attempts to limit China's population growth, is not imposed on them. Thus, the birth-rate among ethnic minorities is more than double that of the Han. (You can find out more about the One-Child Policy on pages 24–25).

7

Changes at Home

The traditional family – two married parents bringing up their children in the family home – is still the most important social unit in China, despite the immense social and economic change of the late twentieth century. Single-parent families are almost unknown.

Are boys worth more than girls?

Chinese society traditionally relied on large families, in which the children helped their parents at work and looked after them in their old age. Boys were especially valued because they could do hard physical work and contribute earnings to the household. Girls were taught to cook, keep house and look after younger children.

In the 1980s the government introduced the One-Child Policy, to try to slow down the growth of China's population. Couples who had more than one child could be punished by losing social benefits or even their jobs. Most parents preferred their one child to be a boy, and there is evidence that many girl babies were killed, especially in country areas. The evidence is supported by the population census of 2000, which showed that males now made up 53 per cent of the population. This was 2 per cent higher than before the One-Child Policy was introduced – and 2 per cent of China's huge population represents millions of people.

Today the One-Child Policy is being relaxed. Rural and ethnic-minority families are unofficially permitted to have

▲ *City streets are never empty. In the evenings and at weekends parents like to take their children out for a stroll.*

larger families. As living standards rise it is becoming less important for parents to have boys to work and provide for them. The terrible crime of infanticide is now showing signs of disappearing.

The relationship between parents and children has been affected by the One-Child Policy. Sixty years ago, the average number of children per family was 6.46. Today the average is 1.44 children. Most Chinese children have neither brothers nor sisters and many grow up never having to consider or learn to get along with others. They expect and demand the latest consumer goods. Chinese sociologists have called these spoiled children 'Little Emperors' because they dominate their families.

▲ *A poster promoting the One-Child Policy. It tells people their standard of living will be better if they have only one child.*

IN THEIR OWN WORDS

'My name is Zhang Cai. I'm a junior school teacher in Danfeng, Shaanxi province. I think that the One-Child Policy has probably made parents more precious about their children. Everyone wants a son, and a lot of these boys are spoiled by their parents. They get everything they want and they don't have to think about a brother or sister. Some of them are actually very lonely. I'm frightened that our communities will start to break down because people don't depend on each other as much as before. As people become more independent they become more selfish. Crime is beginning to increase already, especially in the big cities where all my pupils want to work.'

The teenager arrives in China

Today's young people have opportunities their parents' generation could only dream of – rapidly rising living standards, plentiful consumer goods, more exciting career opportunities, the possibility of foreign travel. Naturally enough, most teenagers want to enjoy what seems to be available to them. The new advertising industry targets young consumers who, as statistics show, are more likely to spend their money than to save it as their parents did. And so what seems like opportunity often becomes pressure – the pressure to buy, to wear the newest designer labels, to own the most sophisticated electronic gadgets, to listen to music and visit clubs and bars. Then there is pressure on parents to earn enough to pay for their children's lifestyle.

IN THEIR OWN WORDS

'I'm Sun Xi (left) and I'm a school student in Shanghai. OK, so I've got crazy hair and a few body piercings. So what? It's no big deal. But my father thinks I'm a disgrace and my headmaster thinks I'm poison! I'm supposed to do nothing but college work so I can get a good job and repay my parents for bringing me up! Just like they did. Five hours a night, five nights a week. But it's not like that now. They give me a monthly allowance but I still can't afford a decent pair of trainers or a mobile phone. All my friends have them. And CD players and computers!'

Despite all the new opportunities available to them, teenagers are still expected to show total obedience to their parents and teachers. There is no tradition of negotiation or discussion between parents and children or teachers and pupils in China. Until the 1990s the idea of teenagers as people developing their own ideas and interests – and occasionally rebelling against authority – was unknown in Chinese families. Many young people complain of a communication gap between the generations.

▶ *Holding hands or kissing in public is becoming a relatively common sight in the cities today, but many older Chinese still think such behaviour is unacceptable.*

IN THEIR OWN WORDS

'I am Professor Rao Dujun, and I am Head of the Foreign Affairs Office in the Provincial Government of Shaanxi. Family life here has undergone tremendous change since the 1980s, but good traditions remain, such as respect for old people. Those who do not respect old people will be strongly criticized. But very few families now live with grandparents and, because children are free to find jobs and settle down in places other than their home towns, not many young people live with their parents. The family plays a very important role in maintaining social stability. Troubled families often produce troubled children. There is no doubt that good family life can keep down the crime rate.'

Food and health

In poorer times obesity used to be a sign of wealth in China; few people could afford enough food to become overweight. However, since 1995 the average calorie intake per person has risen from around 2,700 calories per day to just under 3,000 calories per day. People are eating more sweet and fatty foods (although vegetable-based foods still make up around 80 per cent of the national diet). They are using up less energy at work and on household chores. Despite these changes, obesity-related illness remains rare; more Chinese people die of smoking-related diseases than of illnesses related to their diet.

While smoking fell by 10 per cent in Western countries between 1980 and 2000 it rose in China by over 60 per cent. Among Chinese men there are 300 million smokers – 61 per cent of all Chinese adult males. Cigarette taxes bring in over US$5 billion annually. However the cost to the state as a result of sick smokers being away from work and the additional health care smokers need is around US$8 billion. It is estimated that as many as 50 million Chinese who were children in 2001 will eventually die of smoking-related diseases.

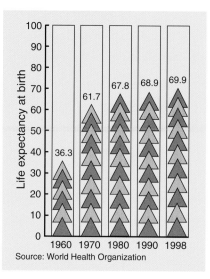

Source: World Health Organization

▲ *Improved life expectancy due to better diets and general health care in the late twentieth century has contributed to the rapid growth of China's population.*

◄ *Families still eat together, although eating patterns are changing. In homes where both parents go out to work, children often eat alone, in front of the TV.*

The Chinese word for 'recipe', *fang*, also means 'prescription' – and making subtle changes to their diet is still the commonest way for Chinese people to treat themselves when they are ill. Foods are categorized as either cooling (*yin*) or warming (*yang*) and a meal is supposed to balance the two. Hot foods include coffee, most meat, heavily processed food and all spicy food. Too much internal heat is said to cause indigestion, skin problems and bad breath, all of which can be 'treated' with cooling foods such as vegetables, most fruit and some fish.

▶ *The fish market in Hong Kong. Fish is an important part of the diet in coastal areas and along bigger rivers, such as the Yangtze.*

IN THEIR OWN WORDS

'I'm Li Yuehui and I live in Xi'an. Some people think that the traditional Chinese medicine I use to treat people is all made from rhino horn or tiger bones or bear paws! Well, I don't use anything like that. Not now. It's supposed to be illegal, anyway. I could get them if I needed them badly. Mostly, I use dried herbs, flowers, roots, berries, fruits and fungi. Ginseng is very important and the best is imported from the United States. Chinese medicine is very good for skin problems, allergies, asthma and sore throats. It is very dusty here and the factory chimneys pour out smoke all day so people have a lot of these problems. I use acupuncture, too, to help restore the body's natural harmony. That's what Chinese medicine's all about.'

What's cookin'?

Chinese food varies from place to place but is usually categorized in four regional cuisines. Northern food includes Beijing duck, and the Mongolian hot-pot (*huo guo*) of boiled slivers of ham with thick vegetable broth. Western or Sichuan food is very hot and spicy. Eastern or Yangtze food uses fish, clear soups and stuffed dumplings (*jiaozi*). Southern or Guangdong (Cantonese) food is best summed up by the southerners themselves, who boast 'We eat anything with four legs, except a table, and anything with wings except an aeroplane.'

▲ *A shop selling different types of tea. Tea is the traditional Chinese drink and in the many teahouses older people, especially, like to linger over a game of cards.*

◀ *Strings of noodles hanging up to dry in the sun.*

IN THEIR OWN WORDS

'I'm Ma Chao, I'm 17 and I live in Luoyang. I've been working since I was three. This food stall is my dad's business (he was a cook in the army) and I used to carry things and collect the bowls when customers had finished. I left school at 13. I was no good at school.

We Chinese made the first fast food. The West only copied – centuries later. Stir-fry and noodles – it just takes a couple of minutes. *Jiaozi* – filled with eggs, leeks and cabbage – better than your mother can make! Very tasty! But maybe we should do hamburgers and hot dogs now. That's what people want if they've tried it in Beijing or Shanghai. People don't have time to sit here and eat any more. They want napkins and fancy boxes to carry their food back to work in. And plastic chopsticks!'

Food is at the centre of family celebrations. Noodles are served at birthdays because their length symbolizes long life. Sweet fruits are served at New Year for good luck. The autumn Moon Festival is the time to enjoy sweet paste-filled moon cakes.

Foreign fast-food restaurants are spreading rapidly in the larger cities. They are very popular with the newly affluent young but there is little sign that they are making a significant impact on the way the Chinese cook and eat.

▶ *Street stalls like this one in Xi'an sell traditional Chinese food. Kiosks selling well-known brands of snacks and soft drinks can also now be found in the cities.*

The Chinese language

Chinese has no alphabet. Words are represented by graphic symbols called 'characters'. Some words use one character; others need several characters to create their meaning. There are probably between 50,000 and 60,000 Chinese characters. The only way to learn them is to memorize them. A well-educated person will know around 10,000 and Chinese children will have memorized around 6,000 by their early teens.

All Chinese dialects use the same printed characters. Therefore, all Chinese read the same language. However, in different parts of the country the same characters are pronounced in entirely different ways. Thus, someone from Beijing may not understand the spoken Chinese of someone from Shanghai or Guangzhou. It is not uncommon to see Chinese people (particularly the elderly) communicating by 'signing' characters on the palms of their hands.

▲ *A newspaper stand in Chengdu. Most towns and villages have communal newspaper boards where local (and some national) newspapers are posted daily and can be read free of charge.*

Standardization

Back in 1956 the government declared the *putonghua* (common speech) dialect of Beijing to be the official spoken form of Chinese for the whole country. A system of representing the common sounds of each character in the Roman alphabet (which is the alphabet used in Western countries) was introduced, called *pinyin*. *Putonghua* and *pinyin* are taught in all schools. Among minority peoples they are sometimes taught as a second language. Today *pinyin* is increasingly used on public signs, at railway stations, in advertising and print.

As China modernizes and develops trade with other countries it becomes increasingly important to be able to communicate simply and efficiently, both internally and externally. *Putonghua* and *pinyin* make it easier to do business in all parts of China, to use the telephone and computers, and to travel for business and leisure purposes.

▲ *University students use the latest educational technology to help them learn foreign languages.*

IN THEIR OWN WORDS

'My name is Jiang Dengzhen. I'm a university teacher in Xi'an. All languages change continuously and Chinese is no different. We have a lot of influences from Western culture – music, burger bars, computers, and so on. We translate them all, but in differing ways. Some are a simple sound 'translation', others are half sound translation and half meaning translation, such as in *yin te wang* [Internet]. *Yin te* means 'inter', and *wang* means 'net'. Some are given a totally Chinese meaning, such as our five-character word for 'modem' which is *tiao zhi jie tiao qi*! In the cities it's not unusual to hear people greet each other with 'Hello!' or 'Hi!' And we don't even try to translate CD, VCR or DVD. *Zai jian*! [Goodbye]'

8

Changes at Work

Cracks in the 'iron rice bowl'

When the Communists took control in 1949, China had been devastated by economic collapse, civil war and political corruption. Desperate times demanded desperate measures. Private land, property and businesses were taken into state control. Farming was collectivized and industry nationalized. Politicians set targets for agricultural and industrial output. In return for the loss of some basic human rights, the Chinese people were offered jobs with guaranteed incomes for life, basic accommodation, rationed food, and schools and health care. These were all provided at the place of work – or 'work unit' – to which they now literally belonged. This Chinese version of a welfare state was known as the 'iron rice bowl' to symbolize the life-long security it offered.

All that is changing fast. To compete in the global economy China has had to make reforms. Collective farming came to an end in the 1980s and farmers are no longer told what or how much to produce. Many now own their own farms again and help run small, highly efficient rural businesses involved in food-processing, handicrafts and tourism.

▼ *Workers laying a new road surface in Guangzhou. Labourers like these are often migrant workers.*

IN THEIR OWN WORDS

'I'm Zhou Yunfang and I work in a factory in Shenzhen. I don't like to be thought of as an economic migrant. I chose to come to Shenzhen because there are plenty of well-paid jobs here. I reckon that three-quarters of the workforce here are, like me, from farming families in Sichuan province, and we all send money back home to our parents every month. In Shenzhen I earn about three times what I could get back in Chengdu.

I work from 7.45 a.m. to 5.45 p.m., six days a week, and I've been making boxes here for six years. I share a couple of rooms with five other girls. We are good friends but we almost never go out. It's too expensive and we're always too tired after work. My dream is to see Hong Kong and visit Shanghai one day.'

People are now allowed to travel within China (although there are still some restrictions) and as many as 100 million have moved to work on building sites or in the rapidly expanding service industries in the cities. Up to a quarter of the population of Guangzhou may be casual workers without adequate housing, sanitation or access to health care or education for their children.

▶ *Some of these traditional Chinese goods are hand-made; others are mass-produced. Tourists are keen to buy such products and large quantities are also exported.*

Made in China

After 1949, nationalization helped to stabilize and develop China's devastated industries. Vital heavy industries such as iron and steel production, coal mining and engineering were re-established. But it was soon clear that state-controlled industries were unprofitable and could not adapt quickly enough to demands for new products. As recently as 1995 they were still unable to supply the growing market within China for well-made consumer goods. Under the 'iron rice bowl' policy, workers had been promised jobs for life but this meant that industries had to employ far more people than they actually required. Change was desperately needed.

The industrial reforms of the 1990s were based on the agricultural reforms introduced in the 1980s by Deng Xiaoping, Mao Zedong's successor. Many state-owned companies were shut down and the newly privatized industries snatched the 'iron rice bowl' from the hands of millions of families. By 2001 urban unemployment had reached 3.2 per cent – still lower than in many EU member states but a level unheard of in China for half a century. Riots and demonstrations against job losses took place in the old industrial regions of northern and central China.

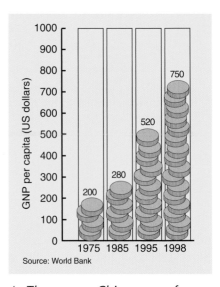

▲ The money China earns from the goods and services it produces has more than trebled since 1975.

◄ A huge cargo ship leaves the docks at Shanghai, escorted by tug boats. The docks were expanded and modernized in the 1980s to allow them to handle the biggest container ships and oil tankers.

IN THEIR OWN WORDS

'I'm Alex Yan and I live in Hong Kong. I was born and educated in Canada and moved here in 1982 to join the family printing business. Today I've got a Ferrari and a helicopter and everything else I want. In this company we export over 90 per cent of what we print to Europe and the US. We can make 5,500 32-page hardback school books an hour. I employ 180 people here and another 600 in Shenzhen, where labour costs are very much lower. In fact, that could be a problem for us. Property prices are falling in Hong Kong as companies move to the Special Economic Zones, like Shenzhen, to take advantage of the cheaper labour there. Over half our employees are single girls from the north. They live together in dormitories and we provide free food and uniforms. They all send money back home.'

Foreign investment and the development of new export markets have made China the world's fastest-growing economy. Economic Development Zones have been set up in the south and many of the businesses there are joint ventures with companies outside China. In these zones, China manufactures clothes, toys and electronic goods for the world. Workers may work long hours for low pay but they are attracted by perks such as the possibility of promotion or of owning a car.

▶ *Printing is now a highly mechanized industry but some jobs are still done by hand. These print workers are pasting covers on to hardback books.*

Tourism

For a quarter of a century, during the regime of Mao Zedong, China was effectively closed to foreign tourists. In the late 1970s political attitudes changed. The state invested heavily in hotel-building and allowed an increased number of international flights into China. Culturally important sites, such as the Great Wall, the Forbidden City in Beijing, the terracotta warriors at the tomb of Qin Shi Huangdi near Xi'an, and the cities of Shanghai and Guangzhou were opened up and developed. However, the tourist industry was still controlled by the state.

At the beginning of the twenty-first century China's foreign tourist industry was rapidly modernized. Joint ventures with foreign hotel and travel chains were encouraged. Foreign investment enabled parts of the Great

▼ *The bright lights of Shanghai attract visitors from within China, as well as foreign tourists.*

Wall to be renovated, and the Forbidden City and other major tourist sites to be refurbished. It also provided funds to build new hotels and airports, and city transit systems such as monorails and metros.

In 2000, over 25 million tourists visited China, mainly from Macau, Taiwan, Japan, Russia, the United States, Singapore, the Philippines and Thailand. Increased prosperity now makes it possible for large numbers of Chinese to travel within their own country. In 2000, over 650 million Chinese travelled in China, an increase of over 50 per cent in five years.

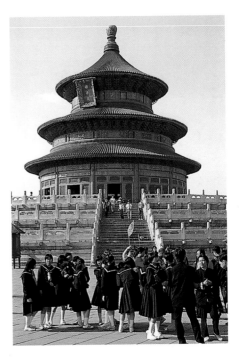

▶ *Visitors in front of the Temple of Heaven, Beijing. Ceremonies were held here during imperial times, to pray for good harvests.*

IN THEIR OWN WORDS

'I'm Sun Yanfeng and I'm a tour guide, based in Beijing. I'm holding this sunflower so everyone in my tour group today can spot me! I speak five languages – Chinese, Japanese, Korean, German and English. Foreign tourism is growing very fast here. I expect there'll always be a job for me. I spend over 75 per cent of my time at work speaking English, not always with native speakers of English. Some nights I even dream in English!

One thing I notice about foreign tourists is that they are almost always very well informed about my country. They ask detailed questions about China's development and especially about the way Chinese families live. They are usually polite but sometimes I get tough questions about human rights in China. So as well as keeping my languages up-to-date I have to make sure I know what's happening here. I keep up with the news and with politics by reading at least three newspapers every day and by making sure I always catch the news on TV or the radio. I have to be able to answer all my clients' questions convincingly and confidently.'

Education for change

China today is modernizing rapidly and the economic changes are providing new jobs for the growing population. By 2001 over 711 million people had jobs – 5 million more than in 1999. Of these, nearly 213 million worked in urban areas – 2.6 million more than in 1999.

Many of the new jobs are low-paid, repetitive and dangerous – health and safety at work is not a priority. Few require workers with much more than basic occupational skills. All, however, require basic levels of literacy. China's education system has struggled to cope with the demand. During 2000 a total of 2.58 million adults completed basic literacy courses. In 1990, 16 per cent of the population was illiterate, but by 2000 that figure had fallen to 7 per cent – still a staggering 86 million people.

By 2000 over 85 per cent of school-age children were in full-time compulsory education. Six years at primary school are followed by three at secondary school. By 2001 over 99 per cent of primary-age children attended school but around 5 per cent drop out and start work – illegally – before secondary school. This tends to happen most often in rural areas. Education provided by the state is supposed to be free, although schools are allowed to charge a small tuition fee – up to £60 per year in urban areas and as little as £4 per year in the countryside.

◀ *Primary school children in a classroom in Xi'an. Schools in urban areas like this tend to be better funded and better equipped than those in country areas.*

Each province has its own curriculum but all pupils take the same highly competitive national college and university entrance exams. The number who pass is relatively small. Those who are successful have the costs of their higher education paid by the state, and after graduating are usually able to move directly into well-paid professional jobs.

▲ *Schoolchildren are encouraged to care for the environment by doing weekly cleaning tasks. These pupils are setting off to pick up litter and sweep the paths around their school.*

IN THEIR OWN WORDS

'My name is Sun Dengxi and I'm studying foreign languages at Shanghai University. I want to work in the import–export business so I have to be able to speak English well. I know more people on the planet speak Chinese, but English is the language of computers. If you're Chinese you have to do business in English or German. Japanese is an important language for us, too. When my father was a student, forty years ago, it was the time of Mao and the Cultural Revolution, and he was arrested and sent to live with peasants in the countryside for eight years – just because he was a student, a hated intellectual. If you had any connections with foreign countries at that time you were 'criticized' by your fellow students – sometimes, even beaten up. It must have been horrible. I don't think that could happen today. We have more contact with foreign countries. China is more open now.'

Another China is born

The Communist Party has a direct influence on everyone's life in China, even though fewer than one in fifty of the population is a party member. It still dictates where most people live, how much they earn, how many children they have and where they can travel. The original aim of all this interference in people's lives was to restore the Chinese virtues of unity, harmony, social order and balance after the upheavals of the first half of the twentieth century. But it also stifled industriousness and creativity and the Chinese love of innovation.

IN THEIR OWN WORDS

'I'm Li Chengao and I'm a taxi driver in Shanghai. I grew up in a work unit in Shenyang. It was a machine-tools factory with about 6,000 employees and we had two drivers – Mr Zhao and Mr Xu. They were very proud of the two factory cars, both black, both huge, both Chinese, of course. They nursed those cars like their own children and when they drove visitors or important guests they wore spotless, white string gloves. No one else knew how to drive. It was a mystery. There were no private cars back then. Mr Zhao and Mr Xu were respected workers.

Things have certainly changed now! Look at me – I'm self-employed with my own air-conditioned, imported car. Thousands of taxis, and hundreds of thousands of private cars all fighting for road space. I guess the traffic's increased by about five times in five years here. My son drives. Even my daughter wants a car. And why not? This isn't Mao's China any more, is it?'

Deng Xiaoping recognized that China needed to change if it was to prosper in the modern world. He introduced the agricultural and industrial reforms of the 1980s and 1990s and another China was born – a China in which the Communist Party itself now has to compete for influence.

◄ *Investors in Xi'an checking the latest stock market figures.*

Private farms and companies need to make profits. They have to be efficient and free to manage themselves, to decide the size of their workforce and promote those with ability. They need a literate workforce with IT skills and – especially in the export and tourism industries – a general knowledge of the world beyond China.

In twenty-first-century China power and influence may be beginning to slip away from the Politburo. In future, power may lie with the men and women who now run China's businesses: the entrepreneurs, media tycoons and entertainment industry celebrities who are driving the new economy and, literally, changing the face of China.

► *The new face of China? Young women play an important role in China's growing media companies.*

9 The Way Ahead

Today, China turns out manufactured goods for the world – but its factories continue to damage the environment. There is increased prosperity but reduced job security. Workers can now change jobs more easily – but risk losing social welfare benefits if they move away from home. Standards of living are rising but so is the crime rate. China willingly embraces new technologies at work – but traditional values are still followed at home. There is a dazzling array of consumer goods to be bought but prices continue to rise beyond the reach of ordinary citizens.

It is a time of unique challenge and opportunity. If the government can tolerate political opposition it will probably maintain political stability at home. It may even improve its poor human rights image abroad. China has never been a democracy. It has a long tradition of strong leadership. However, to retain the support of the people the government will have to use China's new economic wealth to reduce poverty and improve educational opportunity.

▲ *These young people are collecting for charity – a familiar sight in Western cities but a new phenomenon in China, where until recently the state was expected to provide for those in need.*

IN THEIR OWN WORDS

'I'm Chen Zi and I'm a police officer in Guangzhou. China is a very safe country to live in, as long as you're not a criminal – or a police officer on traffic duty! There are lots of police on the streets. We have less crime here because people are scared of us, and I think that's important. People in China respect authority. With all the changes that are taking place though, I'm sure the crime rate will increase, at least in the cities.

Recently a lot of officers have left the police service and joined the private security firms who patrol shopping malls and work for foreign businesses. It's well paid and much easier work, but some of them have already realized how boring it is. They've lost not just their job security but also their status in society. If I work very hard I expect to be a senior detective in less than ten years.'

To secure its role as a superpower China will have to take on more responsibilities in world affairs and carry out its duties more fairly. In 2001 the International Olympic Committee announced that the 2008 Olympic Games would be held in Beijing. For the Chinese government, the Games offer a unique opportunity to improve China's reputation in the international community. China is still seen as reluctant to compromise its Communist principles and dilute its traditional identity in an increasingly global society. However, as Deng Xiaoping himself might have said, you can't have change without change.

▼ *In Tian An Men Square, people celebrate the announcement awarding the 2008 Olympic Games to Beijing.*

Glossary

Acupuncture A traditional Chinese medical treatment, in which needles are stuck into particular parts of the patient's body to relieve pain and other symptoms.

Autonomous region An area of a country that is allowed some freedom to govern itself, instead of being run entirely by the central government.

Calligraphy The art of fine writing of Chinese characters, with brush and ink.

Character A graphic symbol representing a word or part of a word.

Collectivization A process in which a farm, for example, is taken over by the state or a group of workers and the workers share equal responsibility for running it.

Communist A follower of Communism, a political system in which ownership of private property is abolished and all businesses are run by the state on behalf of the people.

Deforestation The cutting down of trees for use in the timber industry or for fuel.

Dynasty A succession of rulers who all belong to the same family.

Fertilizers Substances added to the soil to help plants to grow.

GNP per capita GNP is Gross National Product, the money China makes from all the goods and services it produces. 'Per capita' means per person, so GNP per capita is the total earned, divided by the total population.

Humid Warm and damp.

Huo guo A kind of open kettle, often made of copper. Slivers of meat and chopped vegetables are dipped into the boiling water in the kettle at the table and eaten straight away. It is typical of Mongolian cuisine.

Hydro-electric power Electricity that is generated by using falling water to turn turbines.

Illiterate Unable to read or write.

Infanticide The killing of babies at or soon after birth.

Joint venture (company) A business enterprise in which a Chinese and a foreign company work co-operatively, as one company (foreign companies are currently prevented, by law, from trading directly in China). For example, the foreign company may supply money and technology while the Chinese company provides premises, the labour force and a distribution network.

Lamasery The place where Buddhist monks live; like a monastery in the Christian religion.

Loess Yellow dust-like soil.

Migrant workers Workers who have moved from one area of the country (e.g. a rural area) to work in a different area (e.g. a city).

Nationalization The process of organizing ownership of an industry by the state; a state-owned industry is a nationalized industry.

Nomadic Moving with the changing seasons to find the best food and grazing for animals.

Pesticide A substance used to kill insects that attack crops.

Pinyin The system of representing the sounds of the Western (Roman) alphabet in Chinese.

Politburo The group of senior politicians responsible for policy-making and running the government in Communist states. It is similar to the Cabinet in democratic governments.

Putonghua The official spoken form of modern Chinese (sometimes also known as 'Mandarin Chinese').

Republic A state in which the supreme power is in the hands of the people, or their representative, often called a president.

Revolution The overthrow of the existing government or political system.

Smog A combination of smoke and fog.

Sub-tropical A hot climate, between the temperate and tropical regions.

Temperate A mild climate.

Tropical A very hot, wet climate that occurs in the region between the Tropics of Cancer and Capricorn.

Welfare state A system in which government money is used to provide old-age pensions, unemployment benefits and sickness benefits, so that everybody has a basic income.

Further Information

Books for younger readers

Chinese Cinderella by Adeline Yen Mah (Puffin Books, 1999) This moving autobiography recounts the author's childhood in China during the 1940s and 1950s.

Country Insights: China by Julia Waterlow (Wayland, 2006)

Exploration into China by Wang Tao (Belitha Press, 1995)

Falling Leaves by Adeline Yen Mah (Puffin Books, 1997)

Festivals and Food: China by Amy Sui (Wayland, 2006)

Books for older readers and teachers

A Bend in the Yellow River by Justin Hill (Phoenix, 1998) An evocative account of the author's two years living in central China during the 1990s.

The Drink and Dream Teahouse by Justin Hill (Phoenix Press, 2001) A powerful novel about modern provincial China and the effects of sudden and rapid change. This is not specifically written for young readers. It contains some strong language and images, and some parents/teachers may prefer to read it first before recommending it to their children/pupils.

Hand-grenade Practice in Peking – My Part in the Cultural Revolution by Frances Wood (John Murray, 2000)

Insight Guide China edited by Scott Rutherford et al (APA Publications, 2000 (ninth edition))

Websites

www.atlapedia.com/online/countries/china.htm
www.chinadaily.com.cn
The online version of China's national daily English-language newspaper
Visit learn.co.uk for more resources

Places to visit

The British Museum, London, has a wide-ranging collection of artefacts from Asia.

The Burrell Collection, Glasgow, has a fine collection of ancient Chinese ceramics (including Tang Dynasty horses), bronzes and jades.

China Town, in and around Gerrard Street, in London's West End (off Shaftesbury Avenue, W1), is packed with Chinese businesses. There are smaller 'China Towns' in Manchester and Glasgow. Contact the Tourist Information Centre in each city for details.

The Museum of East Asian Art, 12 Bennett Street, Bath BA1 2QJ has a comprehensive collection of ancient Chinese art.

Useful addresses

Chinese Embassy
49-51 Portland Place
London W1N 4JL
Tel: 020 7299 4049

Consulate-General, Manchester
Denison House, Denison Road
Manchester M14 5RX
Tel: 0161 248 9304

Consulate-General, Edinburgh
Romano House, 43 Station Road
Edinburgh EH12 7AF
Tel: 0131 334 8501

China National Tourist Office
71 Warwick Road
London SW5 9HB
Tel: 020 7373 0888

Stanfords Bookshop
12-14 Long Acre
Covent Garden
London WC2E 9LH
Tel: 020 7836 1321
Fax: 020 7836 0189
e-mail: customer.services@stanfords.co.uk
Probably the finest map and travel bookshop in Britain, with an exhaustive stock of books on and maps of China.

Index

Page numbers in **bold** refer to photographs, maps or statistics panels.